10 WAYS TO MARKET & GROW YOUR BUSINESS WITH ZERO ADVERTISING DOLLARS

Eric Cheng

Kevin Herrera & Angel Poon

12 CREATIVE

Written by Eric Cheng, Kevin Herrera and Angel Poon
Design: Angel Poon

IBSN: 978-1-716-03517-3

TABLE OF CONTENTS

INTRODUCTION

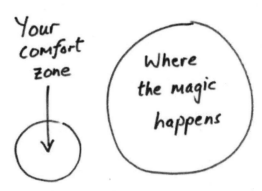

Your comfort zone

Where the magic happens

Hey, we're so glad you made it! Congratulations on taking the first step in growing your business and taking the actionable next steps needed to get started.

In our decades of combined experience, our #1 most frequently asked question has to be, "How do I market and grow my business?" It's an excellent question; in fact, it's probably the main question in every business owner and marketer's mind. To pay it forward, here are our top 10 ways to market and grow your business. We're even going to present each of our points from the perspectives of three different business types, just to make it that much easier for you. We're not saying that you have to implement every one of these strategies. Still, we're confident that at least one of these tactics will help position you and your business for growth.

If you feel uncomfortable with one of our strategies—like starting a vlog—it's time to push your boundaries, move outside your comfort zone and just do it. While not every decision you make has to be a big leap forward (consistent, small baby steps are just as essential), it is conquering new challenges that will truly accelerate growth for you and your business.

Are you ready to take action?

A common complaint we hear is *"this doesn't work for my business"* or *"this doesn't apply to my industry."* While this may be true, and every marketing strategy may not apply to every industry, ideas and methods can be refined to work for you. It's about getting creative!

In this book, we will lead by example, breaking down our ideas and applying them to the three most common industries we encounter: **Service, Retail, and Restaurant.**

SERVICE

Do you serve clients and customers one-on-one by appointments like a dental clinic, hair salon, law firm or accountant? Do you provide a service and your time and expertise for a fee? This section is for you.

RETAIL

Does your business partake in the sale of goods to the public for use? Maybe you are a brick-and-mortar clothing store selling women's apparel, the latest eco-friendly products, or sporting goods? Or perhaps you choose to operate in an online e-commerce marketplace? Either way, this section is for you.

RESTAURANT

Do you own the neighbourhood's favourite pizza joint? Your own ice cream franchise? Maybe you do marketing for the local coffee shop and hipster hangout? If you are feeding people in one way or another, this section is for you.

These businesses are, as we call, Business to Customer (B2C). For those of you who operate Business to Business (B2B), we're sure you can still refine some of the upcoming strategies to better serve your needs, but if you want more information, shoot us an email at **contact@12creative.co**. We would love to hear from you!

THE 5 W'S

Before we dive into the guts of marketing strategy, we like to start by asking: **Who? What? Where? When? And Why?**

These simple questions are the best, most essential questions to ask any client before diving into strategy. The 5 W's are deviously simple yet crucially important to ask as they reveal goals and obstacles that you otherwise might not have previously thought of or encountered. So take a moment, step back, reflect and start asking yourself, Who? What? Where? When? And Why?

To get you started, here are a few key questions you should ask yourself:

- **Who** is my audience?

- **Who** do I serve, and how do I provide value to them?

- **What** are the problems that I am trying to solve?

- **What** feelings do I want to invoke in my customers before, during and after engaging with my business?

- **What** are my goals?

- **What** purpose am I serving? (to my clients and my community)

- **What** is my action plan?

- **Where** can I continue to grow my business?

- **When** do I want to accomplish my goals by?

- **Why** did I start my business or job?

Twelve Tip!
Set measurable milestones and goals with action steps in place. If you had to break down your goals into only five achievable steps, what would they be? Write it down and schedule it into your daily calendar.

Lastly, **you've got to believe it to achieve it.** Have a vision of what your business and your life will look like when you achieve your goal...now write that down!

A GOAL IS A DREAM WITH A DEADLINE.

THE FORMULA IS SIMPLE.
EDUCATE, ENTERTAIN
AND INSPIRE.

CHAPTER 1
THE LISTENING EXPERIENCE
Start a Podcast

In our modern-day of short hair, short pants and even shorter attention spans, people are always looking for new forms of entertainment, introducing Podcasts! The perfect platform to not only entertain but also educate.

What's so special about podcasts, and why should I care? Podcasts allow you to create your own on-demand talk radio, and you should care because experts estimate that the podcast industry will be a whopping $70.5 billion industry in the year 2021—that's a lot of people listening to podcasts! A few decades ago, the traditional methods of getting people to have a listening experience (LX) were much more cumbersome and complicated. It involved hiring others to produce an original ad, purchasing radio ad time and then hoping someone out there would be listening to your specific radio station at your exact purchased time! Not to mention, the listener also has to remember to engage with your brand afterwards. Let us be the first to remind you that **those days are over**! Today, we live in a time where we can create our own media, shows, and podcasts, driving our listeners to our content wherever and whenever they please. Whether people are cooking, running, at the gym, driving, or doing the laundry, podcasts allow businesses to provide LX and content to their listeners at their convenience. Spotify and Apple have invested millions in growing their listeners and getting folks like you and us to listen to their content in recent years. Podcast Celebs, like Joe Rogan, have inked 100 million dollar deals with Spotify, and the list goes on. However, this is only the beginning of it.

So why should one create a podcast, either for themselves or their business? Think of it as creating your own radio show. The Topic? Anything you want! But hopefully, something somewhat related to your business/industry. The key is to create something of interest to bring valuable content to the (potential) customer and bring awareness to yourself and your brand. Instead of buying radio ads, build your own radio show where your audience tunes into. The ads on your podcast can be friends and other businesses that bring your business value. **Podcasts help you build Brand Value!**

GOOD COMPANIES HAVE CUSTOMERS, GREAT COMPANIES HAVE AN AUDIENCE.

Imagine a group of loyal followers that tune in for every release of your latest episode. The more entertaining your show is, the more value it brings listeners, resulting in more listeners wanting to engage with your brand. Think of your company as NBC / CNN / GLOBAL or CBC. Your company is a media company with an audience, and the podcast is one of your shows.

Podcasts can unite communities, provoke thoughtful conversations and educate individuals looking to learn more about your topic of choice. One great way to narrow your audience is to think about the demographics of your audience, what they do for work and how they play. Your show topic also doesn't have to only be about work. For example, your business sells high-end home renovations, and it just so happens that most of your past clients also love to play golf. Perhaps it's time to create your city's best Golf Podcast, brought to you by...your home reno company, listed and mentioned as the key sponsor, of course! Remember, **be where your audience is.**

SERVICE

You run the neighbourhood dental clinic. No, you don't have to create a podcast about the ins and outs of dentistry or your favourite flossing techniques. Think about your clients and what they care about.

Most likely, your clinic serves your community, so your primary focus is to bring in more patients residing in your area. How can you shine more light on your community and bring more listeners in from your surrounding area? If your business is service-based, create a podcast featuring guests and businesses within your community. Try interviewing the owners of the local coffee shop, the principal of the neighbourhood school or your local politician. Ask them about their journeys, life and why they love the area. From there, you can begin to expand your reach to other neighbourhoods and eventually the rest of your town/city! Remember to have fun with it, and don't forget to post the episodes on your website and social media! You can also ask all your interviewees to share your podcast on their websites/socials. This simple request will direct further traffic back to you and your business and is a great way to meet new people and grow your network.

Twelve Tip!
Don't just record audio; also record video! You can then turn your episodes into vlogs and have easily accessible video content. You can also use video as an opportunity to showcase your business. Can you use your waiting area as a perfect backdrop for the recording studio of your podcast?

RETAIL

You are a local specialized upscale women's clothing boutique. You want to create a podcast, but you don't know where to start.

Here are a few topic ideas:

- Try doing an interview series with fellow female entrepreneurs and leaders. Focus on their journeys and struggles, and discuss how they got to where they are today. You could begin by highlighting local entrepreneurs and sharing their stores. Once your interview is complete, encourage your interviewees to share the podcast on their social platforms. This simple gesture will not only drive traffic back to your business/website, but now your brand will reach a new audience of potential customers.

- What about a podcast series talking about the origin story behind each of the brands your business carries? Why do you love the brands enough to have them in your store?

- Call upon the local fashionistas and bloggers. Discuss the impacts of fast fashion, the prevalent fashion trends, what role style plays in their lives, and their fashion tips! These individuals may have an extensive reach so you may be thinking: "do I have to pay them to come onto my show?" In most cases, no. But if they do ask, have them come into the store, and perhaps you can exchange services by providing them with a couple of pieces or an outfit they can show off on their Instagram. Either way, it's a win-win for both parties!

Twelve Tip!
Transcribe each episode to a blog post that lives on your website, if you don't have time to do so, use an employee, online service, or virtual assistant to do so. You can use as site like https://www.rev.com/ or find a freelancer on upwork.com)

RESTAURANT

You own the local pizzeria and are looking to grow and market your business to get more walk-in traffic during the slower times of the week.

Here are some ideas to bring you some sure-fire traffic:

- Create a series that talks to local foodies or food bloggers! Ask them pertinent questions like what their favourite go-to restaurants are, how they grew to become a food blogger, and what their favourite dishes to make at home are. By doing so, not only are you exposing your brand to more foodies, but you are also leveraging their audience when they tweet, share or post about their interview on your show. In any city, there will be no shortage of food bloggers.

Twelve Tip!
Use Instagram hashtags (#) to search for local foodies in your city.

- Highlight local sports teams, coaches, star athletes and young athletes. When was the last time a pizza shop hosted the largest local homegrown sports talk show? Have your interviews in your pizzeria and take a photo with each athlete holding a slice of your specialty pizza or pizza box. As the photo gets shared on their social media and website, so will your brand. Additionally, invite the teams and their families to come by our shop on game days for a game day discount!

Twelve Tip!
Create/name a pizza after different local star athletes. Have the pizza feature their favourite toppings and then promote the pizza on special or as part of your secret menu for the month. Said star athlete will tell all their friends and family to visit your restaurant, promoting your business.

- Interview other restaurant owners. While you might think this may do more harm than good, it's the opposite! By interviewing other local restaurants, you'd be able to "piggyback" on those restaurants' fans and build a good rapport with your city and the local areas you serve. To name a few other topics up for discussion: ask fellow restaurant industry members about their food, what they love, what a day in the life of running a restaurant business looks like and what their favourite dish is (when not eating in their own restaurant, of course).

CHAPTER 2
YOU ARE A MEDIA COMPANY
Create a Video Series

YouTube has 2 billion logged-in monthly users, with 73% of adults and 81% of teens (aged 15-18) claiming to use its services in the US. By 2022, online videos will make up 82% of all consumer traffic.

With 81% of businesses using video marketing as a tool, we have to ask ourselves how companies use video marketing to gain the most attention. **How can you use video for your business?**

An entertaining strategy we love to recommend is getting into video. As Instagram Reels, YouTube, TikTok, and other similar platforms suggest, moving images are increasingly preferred over still ones. Moreover, as we have previously mentioned, we live in a time where it couldn't be easier to create one's own videos and shows. No more investing millions of dollars in writing a pilot script, hiring a production team, or pitching to a major network! Just grab a camera (or smartphone), connect yourself to the Internet, hit upload and publish and wow! Look at that, you have yourself a show! It's that easy.

Let's once again think of your business as a media company. Your podcast can be one show, while this new video series can be another. Think of it as your own TV Show with no limit on the length of each episode or how many episodes per season. And instead of having your show live on a TV channel only accessible during your prepaid airtime, your video series can live on your website or on popular video sharing sites like Vimeo and YouTube for convenient watching anywhere and anytime! While a podcast focuses on creating a listening experience (LX), a video series focuses on creating a visual experience (VX). Different audiences prefer different forms of content and media through different social channels. Your business needs to be in each one to further your reach and maintain relevance. Video is another great way for the audience to engage with you and your brand.

Can you create a weekly live show on Facebook / Instagram / LinkedIn showing the behind-the-scenes of what goes into your business? Don't want to go LIVE? No problem! Record your videos ahead of time and then do a timed-release instead. Try creating an interview series, a lineup of tips and tricks, showcase how your product is made or talk about your business journey. The possibilities are endless, only limited by your drive and effort.

Read below for samples of how you can incorporate a video series into your marketing efforts to grow your brand and build your audience. Remember, YouTube is used widely as a search engine. So think of **"How To Videos"** if you can help it. E.g. How to Change a Car Battery, How to Bake Bread, How to Hem Pants...etc.

SERVICE

You own a physiotherapy clinic, and you're looking for more ways to solidify your brand, knowledge and authority in the marketplace. Additionally, you are looking to grow your client base to hopefully hire more therapists and eventually open multiple locations.

Create a series focusing on the most common injuries and how to prevent them by doing daily exercises at home. This series can consist of diet tips, preventative stretches, and simple rehab techniques. Your series could also include easy at-home or gym workouts, focusing/isolating different muscle groups. People love easy-to-do guides and tutorial shows, so keep things short and simple! Don't forget, always ask yourself: what problem am I solving for our clients? A good starting point is to think about your clients' most commonly asked questions and try answering them through video.

Another idea is to upload a series on your website to allow viewers to book a consultation with your clinic. There is a good chance that when they are ready to receive one-on-one professional treatment after watching your videos, you will be the one they call. Remember, you are building a brand!

Twelve Tip!
Use snippets of the videos you make for social content on your on Instagram, Facebook, TikTok and even LinkedIn.

RETAIL

You own a locally based men's clothing boutique, and you want to grow your business within your city.

Try creating a round table show at your store after hours. Invite locals to come in for a conversation about life, the city, and culture, and afterwards, they can choose to be styled or not. The key here is to build brand recognition and awareness, not sell. Perhaps you could create weekly style guide videos. Invite friends, customers, models and influencers to come in and be styled in the latest outfits. No matter what you choose to do, try to invite different guests to expose you to diverse audiences. When guests share your videos, your brand will reach new audiences, each with its own unique tastes and styles.

Collaborate with other local businesses and showcase products that might go together. For example, team up with the local barbershop and highlight a specialty hair product, the perfect go-to pairing to get ready for a first date. If you find yourself stuck, think like you're GQ magazine. **What would you fill the pages with?**

Several other fun ideas include: reviewing style trends of the season, lookbooks for particular events (e.g. first date, job interviews, night out) and common styling mistakes, to name a few.

RESTAURANT

You are a restaurant owner. No matter the cuisine, this is the perfect opportunity to showcase behind-the-scenes or make some of your signature items. People love "open kitchen concepts," which can mean many things. We have seen a ton of success from cooking or food-related shows on YouTube and Netflix. E.g. Anthony Bourdain's *"Parts Unknown"* or Andrew Rea's *"Binging with Babish."* Everyone loves watching a good show about food!

Here are a few ideas to get you started:

- Create a series showcasing the making of some signature dishes in your restaurant. E.g. how the pasta is made, what market the fresh ingredients come from, how ingredients are chosen, what goes into the dish, your chef making each of the dishes. Have new episodes released weekly on YouTube and Facebook (don't forget to repost clips on Instagram and TikTok).

- Invite bloggers and social media influencers to come in for a meal and cocktails, then have a round table open conversation about your city, life, travel and culture.

- Create a show about the day in the life in your restaurant. If you can, include your family and staff for a more personable feel. Think of this as your own reality show where you can go in behind the scenes and talk about your journey in creating and building the restaurant. Additionally, you can show your day-to-day operations, hardships and wins.

- Host a cooking show in your kitchen and teach your audience how to make certain foods from home. You can even mention some of your favourite local go-to farmer's markets and grocery stores to pick up fresh ingredients. The show can be accompanied by a downloadable recipe book. We suggest making a print version and selling it to a restaurant if it takes off! Maybe proceeds from the book go towards your local favourite charity of choice.

CHAPTER 3
GIVE VALUE FIRST

"Jab Jab Jab, Right Hook" - Gary Vaynerchuk

In today's business world, we are constantly asking for something from our customers. Businesses ask customers to look at their products, to like their photos, promote their products, share their socials and spend money. *"Look at this sale! Buy this product to solve your problems! Wear this to look beautiful!"* The problem with today's economy is that **people go in for *"the ask"* too early.** We think it's about time businesses began representing themselves in a totally different way.

Think of impressing your potential customers like impressing a potential romantic partner. You notice them from across the room, or perhaps you've stumbled across their profile while browsing social media. After this brief first encounter, it's improbable that you're going to approach them and then drop down on one knee to propose. That's a massive ask with no foundation to stand on! **Business is similar to romantic relationships.** We have to consider the value that is added to our lives and think about whether or not it is worth our invested time, money and efforts. In romantic relationships, we build up our trust and learn more about our partners over time by going on dates. While we don't exactly "date" our potential customers in business, we still have to think about how, when, and where we can display information about ourselves. **We have to show individuals that we can solve their problems, make their lives easier and even educate and entertain them.** These are necessary steps before asking for any sort of commitment (sales).

The great thing about putting out valuable content or offering free trials is building out your marketing list—build a strong list of warm or potential customers down the road.

Some examples of methods to get your content out there include:

- Building an email marketing list through email newsletters

- Give away a free mini ebook filled with advice, tips and tricks

- Create free trial offers

- Offer potential clients complimentary consultations, sessions or discovery meetings

- Offer free tours

- Create a free video training series

- Host a webinar

- Write a blog

- Write a book

- Write articles for a blog or publication, offline or online

- Be a guest on a podcast or video series in your industry

A great resource we have drawn inspiration from is Gary Vaynerchuk's *Jab, Jab, Jab, Right Hook: How to Tell Your Story in a Noisy Social World* (we are not sponsored, we're just big fans of his work). His book offers similar insights and much more, acting as a blueprint to many other social media marketing strategies.

SERVICE

You're a fitness trainer. How might you begin providing your clients with value first?

- Create a how-to guide for daily stretches at home

- Create a how-to guide to creating a 7-day workout/meal schedule

- Offer a free virtual or in-person one-on-one 30 min physical assessment quiz

- Create a free video series featuring the top 3 workouts for each of the different muscle groups to do at home and or at the gym

- Create a video series showcasing "apartment-friendly" workouts to do from home

- Create a blank monthly meal/workout calendar template that people can download and fill

- Create a complimentary clean eating shopping list guide (often diet and shopping for the diet can be the most challenging part)

RETAIL

You own a unisex apparel company. In what ways can you add value to your customers' lives?

- Create a downloadable seasonal lookbook

- Create a podcast and talk about the evolving fashion industry or upcoming trends for the seasons

- Have a monthly newsletter featuring various styling tips (you can showcase your products here too)

- *"How to wear _____"* guide in the form of a video series or booklet on your website and socials

- Fashion Education, e.g. jean boot cut, straight leg, tapered and shoes that match the best with those types of jeans.

- Build a magazine showcasing local businesses and those that align with yours

- Promote local business around you and your neighbourhood.

RESTAURANT

- Free cookbook—who doesn't love a good cookbook?

- Weekly "try at home" recipes in a newsletter

- *"How to Make our Favourite Dish at Home"* video series

- Complimentary wine tasting night

   Twelve Tip!
   Try and get this sponsored by your liquor suppliers

- Complimentary tasting night and open house

- Host a cooking class or classes

- Complimentary dessert with a free dinner voucher

- Appetizer voucher for the next meal

CHAPTER 4
THROW THE PARTY
Host an Open House or Workshop

There is something to be said about the in-person EXPERIENCE. In our rapidly changing online, digital world, those live in-person interactions are often forgotten about. An in-person experience can not be replicated through social media, videos or photos. Expose your brand by creating memorable experiences. There's no better way to do that than by bringing people in the door.

Workshops not only provide valuable knowledge and expertise, but they also provide a perfect networking opportunity for those attending.

SERVICE

Try hosting an open house or an information session. This is a great way to thank your current customers. By having them invite their friends and family, you retain your existing customers and simultaneously introduce your brand to newcomers. You can also reach out to the community to bring new potential customers to your complimentary information session or open house event.

TIPS FOR HOSTING AN OPEN HOUSE

So you want to host an open house? Try hosting an open house on a weekday evening (like a Thursday)! It will be more convenient for friends, family and potential clients to attend after work rather than accommodating on their weekends. Here are a few more tips to help your open house run smoothly:

- Have an itinerary and stick to it

- Make sure your guest speaker(s), if any, are kept in the loop

- Prepare a "thank you for coming" speech (keep it short and sweet)

- Provide a photo backdrop for photo opportunities and sharing on social media

- Coordinate food and drinks (can you get these sponsored by local businesses? If yes, don't forget to acknowledge them in your thank you speech!)

- Small takeaways/giveaways - people love swag bags (check out swagup.com)

- Find local business partners, neighbours or vendors to help sponsor gifts, entertainment, or guest speaker at your event.

- Coordinate your event rentals ahead of time and rental pick up for when the event is complete

RETAIL

Open houses are workshops are wonderful ways for people to meet, socialize, be entertained and connect with like minded people. As a physical retail store your opportunities are endless. You have the perfect setting to open your doors to the world. Further unlock your store's potential by becoming a venue and attracting new shoppers to visit.

When planning your event, think outside of the box past the usual food and boozy drinks! Why not look into:

- Bringing in special features (like a photo booth or pretzel wall)

- Hosting a fashion show and inviting local celebrities and fashion bloggers

- Hosting a charitable event where a set portion of sales are donated to a charity of your choice

- Making it an educational night where industry leaders, vendors and/ or professionals come to speak about their products

- Hiring a local band for some live entertainment

One event not enough? We agree. Why not host multiple events over the course of a weekend! For example, the main event/party can be hosted on a Friday and then for the rest of the weekend you can carry out other promotions to encourage more people to come to visit.

Hold on—you're an e-commerce retail and don't have a physical location you say? No problem! All of the above can still be done, it just takes a little more creativity. Collaborate with another fellow retailer and see if they would be interested in sharing their space for the time of the event(s). Eg. You sell pet products, so you team up with a pet groomer to sell your wares in their salon. There is also great opportunity for e-commerce retailers to rent an empty space to create a limited time pop up shop/event. This is especially great as your fans, who are used to an online shopping experience, don't usually get to meet in a physical space and interact with you or your team in person. This unique opportunity can be an annual event you host.

Twelve Tip!

Make it an annual special event. Whether it be an open house, special friends and family sale, make it something special that your audience will look forward to attending. Find event sponsors such as local breweries to help supply or discount your cold ones in exchange for product and/or signage opportunities.

RESTAURANT

In the restaurant/food service industry, hosting a workshop or open house might be hard. Your hours are more sporadic as business can be unpredictable at times, but there are alternative ways to get folks into your doors.

Try hosting menu tastings when you reveal new menu items or featured seasonal items. Keep these tastings exclusive with only a limited number of spots people can reserve. This will help generate feelings of excitement and anticipation for your customers—who doesn't love feeling exclusive? Menu tastings are also a great opportunity for feedback.

Why not try booking an open house or cooking class on slower days or when you're closed. This way, you'll have more time to prepare for the special event(s) and drive traffic in on an otherwise quiet business day.

Twelve Tip!
Film the cooking classes and upload them on YouTube! This provides customers and followers with content to watch whenever they want (as we've previously mentioned, provide value first).

Here are a few more ideas to get you started:

- Host cooking classes (You can theme these, i.e. Valentine's Day Cooking Class)

- Drinks and tapas open house for VIP clients, friends and family

- Menu Tastings or launches with content creators (influencers)

- Cocktail Workshops

- Host paint nights and include food/drinks

- Host a fundraiser for a local charity of your choice with 100% of proceeds going towards the cause.

CHAPTER 5

THE CELEBRITY ENDORSEMENT

Hire Influencers and Content Creators

Word of mouth is one of the strongest forms of marketing. There is a reason why reviews hold so much power, we trust the words and opinions shared by others. It is why influencer marketing has taken the marketing industry by storm.

89% say the return on investment (ROI) from influencer marketing/content creators is comparable to or better than other marketing channels. Over the past decade, the drastic growth in the influencer marketing industry has transformed itself from being a developing marketing method to a multi-billion dollar sector of the global marketing industry. (This is why Kylie Jenner has been paid up to 1.2M for a single post on Instagram!)

Influencer marketing takes someone influential in a specific social community or niche. It uses its platform to appeal to its audience. In other words, you are using the influencers' words to market to their audience. It's similar to hiring a celebrity and endorsing your product/service. However, unlike prominent celebrity endorsements, the influencer or content creator you hire can have a specific group of followers, target a particular niche market, and be a low-cost or no-cost collaboration.

These partnerships can come in many shapes and sizes, and some of these content creators may also already be big fans of your product or brand. They can also create a continual campaign through partnership deals such as promo, referral codes or an ambassador program.

Hiring content creators are the new way to tap into Word of Mouth marketing. Another reason influencer marketing works so well is because influencers seem more approachable than your average A-list or B-list celebrity. People see more of themselves in influencers, especially those who aren't living outwardly lavish lifestyles. There is already a connection or relationship to that person. If you do your research correctly, not only are you tapping into a new market, you are tapping into a concentrated audience that might already be interested in your product.

Before you hire your first (or next) influencer, here are some tips that will help the interaction go smoothly:

- The larger the following, the more likely an influencer will charge.

- Not all influencers necessarily have the strongest audience. Be sure to ask to see an influencer's metrics before working with them. Find brands they have worked with before and ask how the experience went.

- Follower count isn't everything! If you are interested in hiring a content creator, look at their post engagements (likes and comments). Are the comments authentic, part of an engagement pod, or does the influencer have fake followers? These are important things to keep in mind when researching influencers.

- You can usually tell if they are part of an engagement pod if they have generic and similar comments from the same groups of people on all of their posts
    » Who is taking the photo? (Do you have to hire a photographer?)
    » Who or what will be in the photo?
    » How many photos, stories, video/reels, TikTok, and blogs will be posted?
    » When will content be posted? How long will it stay up?
    » Who will be tagged and mentioned in the photo
    » Are you allowed to use the image in our post and /or ongoing ads, and for how long?
    » How or when do you accept payment
    » What will the caption be of the post?

Twelve Tip!

Micro-influencers (10K followers or less) can help you market niche products/ services.

SERVICE

Collaborate with influencers by providing an exchange of products/services. Your exchange can act as a form of payment for the post(s) on your selected influencer's account. If necessary, it can be even more than one exchange to provide equal value.

If you own a service-based business, you can trade influencer posting for free or discounted services. Some examples can be nails, hair, massage, fitness classes and more. The exchange will act as a form of payment for the posting. You may also try offering discounted services/codes. For example, for every person who shows you the Instagram post in which you collaborated with the influencer, Jane Smith, they get 10% off their next first massage session.

Another strategy that works is creating an ambassador or partnership program. There is an ongoing benefit to the influencer while continually promoting your service. This can be set up with a monthly agreement, yearly agreement, or even a kickback referral program. E.g. Lindsay will continue to get 1 free massage per month - as long as she refers "x" amount of people to the clinic and posts 1 time per month. For every 10 people, Lindsay refers she will also receive $250.

RETAIL

For retail the model is easy, trade your products or provide a discount for influencer services. This can apply to most products. You can also take advantage of the connections you have. For example, if you have a clothing retail store and know some photographers that constantly need wardrobes, give them access to your inventory so that you can get more content and exposure and they can have access to the wardrobes they need.

Many of these photographers can be considered influencers as they have a micro-influencer following and always promote their content on social platforms. Another easy way to work with influencers is getting them to model for you and using this as content on your websites and social media, depending on your agreement they will likely do the same.

RESTAURANT

Hire some influencers to come to a tasting dinner, VIP event, or partner for a giveaway. A food blogger always needs content, and they live to review the newest restaurants and hidden gems. Find a list of influencers you can reach out to and coordinate the following activations with them.

Food bloggers are always on the lookout for new content. They thrive on reviewing the latest restaurants, latest food trends and showcasing hidden gems. Find a list of influencers you can reach out to and try coordinating one of the subsequent activations with them:

- Tasting dinners are great opportunities to introduce your restaurant to people who can spread the word and create great social media and photo/video opportunities.

- Drinks and tapas open house for VIP clients, friends and family

- Giveaways - partner with them to do a giveaway

- Giveaways - partner with them to do a giveaway
    - » Win a free meal(s) or gift cards
    - » Complimentary upgrades (appetizers, drinks, desserts...)

Twelve Tip!
Find food bloggers through google or searching the #"city" food hashtag in your local area, then click on TOP and browse the top users and their posts.

CHAPTER 6
SUCCESS IN PARTNERSHIPS

"We're all working together—that's the secret" - Sam Walton

In the digital age filled with friends, followers, subscribers and connections, you begin to realize it's a small world! Everyone knows somebody, so it's essential to foster and build strong relationships/partnerships within your industry. You never know when you'll need someone else's expertise within your industry.

When thinking of partnerships or alliances, keep in mind that every business has its own strengths and weaknesses. Can their strengths balance out some of your weaknesses?

Work on supporting your fellow business owners so you can both succeed, rather than using fierce competition tactics to tear them down and give you a bad reputation. Building partnerships don't always have to be within your industry either. Look into creating alliances that will help you cross-promote and build your brand across industries.

Benefits of Strategic Alliances

- Access to supplementary services

- Newmarket opportunities

- Increased Brand Awareness

- Access to new customer base

Maybe the business alliance is something people didn't know they wanted or needed. For example, Canadian ice creamery **Made by Marcus** and their famous **Espresso & PB&J** ice cream collaborated with **Transcend Coffee**, a local coffee shop and Roastery. If you didn't know about Transcend, now you do! Made by Marcus doesn't specialize in making coffee, so they partnered with the right people to make their ice cream taste better. Another bonus is that they collaborated with another local business! **Think: who has my clients?**

E.g. If you want to market to restaurants owners, why not build a partnership with restaurant suppliers? If you specialize in dental websites, explore options to partner with dental equipment sales representatives to spread the word?

SERVICE

Partnerships operate like a two-way street. It's a bit give and take from both sides. Work with your partnerships and give each other referrals. Not only will this help your business grow, but it will also help your partner's business grow too!

You can also collaborate through giveaways! This could look like a bridal relaxation package courtesy of a local spa and nail salon. Why not go the extra mile and partner with a retail store as well?

Partnership & Giveaway Ideas:

- **Formal Boutique x Hair & Makeup Studio** – when you buy a dress from the Formal Boutique, you get 15% off on a hair & makeup package at the partnered studio.

- **Apartment Complex x Automobile Shop** – when you show your mechanic you live in the partnered apartment complex, you get 10% off their products and services.

- **Wedding Venue x Travel Agency** – You will receive a $500 credit towards your honeymoon at the travel agency when you book your wedding with us.

RETAIL

You can create a retail partnership with brick and mortar and other ways. Suppose you don't have a physical location and are looking to partner with someone. In that case, you can create opportunities you wouldn't have had otherwise. You want to find a partner that has a shared audience but does not compete directly with your business.

An example would be a coffee shop partnering with a florist - people will come for coffee, see flowers and house plants, and maybe buy a plant for their home. People will also do the same when they come in to buy plants. They will likely grab a drink to go once they have bought their plants.

Another example that we see often but can be translated to multiple businesses is creating a **market event**. Partner with other retailers and set up a market event at your business. Companies will set up their tables and sell their products. This will help you establish partnerships with many companies.

Events can also come in the form of **pop-up shops**. If you are a brand and would like to use retail space, partner with one of your stockists to borrow their space. This will allow you to promote your pop-up shop and bring foot traffic to your retail partner.

RESTAURANT

There are many creative ways you can build partnerships when you're in the restaurant business. Partner with other local businesses in your community and provide discounts—create a "Business Lunch Special". You can also collaborate with other restaurants to host events and parties. Perhaps the local brewery will partner with your restaurant for a fun tasting event! Have fun with it and think of ways to market to different audiences. This way, you can broaden your reach and diversify your clientele.

Partnership Ideas:

- Host Networking Events / Conference Dinners

- Meal specials for community workers

- Local winery/wine importer pairing and tasting menu

- Bakeshop provides all the bread and/or deserts in your restaurant

- Pop-ups in breweries or wine bars

- Guest Chef specials

- Locally grown foods

CHAPTER 7

YOUR NETWORK IS YOUR NET WORTH

Build a Network

Whether in-person or online, building a networking group can be beneficial for your business and help position you as a leader in your industry. Networking groups provide a safe space for business owners to connect with people who share similar passions, interests, pains and problems. They allow for fellow industry members to collaborate and connect. While industry-specific networking groups do not market your business directly to potential customers, they can create strong bonds and push your brand awareness while simultaneously establishing yourself as a leader in your industry.

Networking groups don't have to only be for industry members, it can be a place for customers and consumers! Not keen on creating a group of your own? You can always join existing groups on Facebook or in your community. Use a pre-established platform to share your business.

Think about **podcasts** that create exclusive **Discord** groups where you can access exclusive content. This is a great way to build a networking group and a place for your dedicated followers and audience to build community. Creating a group is one of the easiest ways to build connections in the community or with like-minded individuals. You can use the fantastic tools at hand, such as Facebook groups, to create a space to invite others with common interests.

Let's say you are a real estate agent, but you are also a dog lover! Try creating a group online for local dog owners and host meet-ups. This is a fantastic opportunity to meet people with the same interests but, of course, introduce your business or service. It just so happens dog owners also live in.

Create a group for your favourite hobbies, local events, provide small business help and support. The ideas are endless, but just because you are a real estate agent doesn't mean you need to create a group about buying and selling homes.

SERVICE

In many practices, your customers have to do work at home on their own time, such as brushing and flossing - dental, and stretches and exercises (physio), to name a few. Try creating an online social group where you host resources to help your clients/customers with their "homework." Encourage group members to discuss their experiences, challenges and achievements.

If you are a physio clinic, this is the perfect way to build a community, create a group for people who want to stay in shape. In this place, you and your team can share tips and tricks, exercises and answer questions for free. The group you create can host free videos that only your group has access to. Your group will develop and build a community of individuals who are not only looking for more information but can meet each other.

Your exclusive Facebook group will let you build a warm audience and a group of potential customers without even visiting your physical location. When they are ready to seek help, you know they will be calling you.

Twelve Tip!
Turn your educational resources and videos into a digital course or product that can be purchased by your raving fans in the group. This will allow you to take the geographical restrictions out of your business and reach anyone in the world.

RETAIL

Subscription shopping is at an all-time high. People want convenience, and if your product can provide that, you can create a club. Entice membership of the club by promoting special perks for members–first access, special products, discounted prices, and more!

Take a look at companies like **ASYSTEM** skincare from Los Angeles, which provides subscription skincare, or **IPSY**, a monthly subscription service that provides subscribers with a makeup bag of five cosmetics samples based upon users' preferences. Customers who participate in Wine clubs get lower prices and benefit the wineries as they can make higher margins on their products.

Starting a club can help you build your brand's culture and a loyal following. It can also give you something more to market. Clubs will not be your only offering, but they can be very appealing for specific audiences.

If you are a local liquor store, be the wine expert in your city by hosting a Facebook group for wine connoisseurs and a panel of local experts. Fans can share their wine, have online wine tasting events and ask questions.

RESTAURANT

Be a leader in your industry by creating a support group for other restaurants in your community. Create a space where colleagues can talk about shared problems or frustrations and help each other find solutions. You can also use network groups to share exciting opportunities with your industry friends.

What about creating a dinner club? Dinner clubs allow people to meet each other and bond over evenings filled with food and drink. Invite a wide variety of people to the dinner club as it can yield positive word-of-mouth marketing for your restaurant. A dinner club can also increase your service offering and give you additional content to promote on your social media channels. If you are a restaurant with a rotating menu or seasonal menu, use your dinner club as an opportunity for feedback. Test all of your new menu items with the dinner club!

This dinner club can be accessible only to members of your online group. This requires your audience to join to be part of something special. If your group grows quite large, you can begin doing draws for the monthly dinner club or access to hidden menus. Keep it entertaining!

CHAPTER 8
THE ALMIGHTY EXCHANGE
How to Leverage Exposure Through Branding

Traditional methods of marketing-days-past included taking out an ad in the local newspaper, magazine or dropping off flyers (our CEO, Eric, did this for years). If you were so fortunate enough, you could afford to buy some air time on TV or radio. Nowadays, we are lucky to have access to endless free resources and marketing tools like social media networks, online communities and chat rooms. In other words, **nowadays we can promote our businesses for FREE**.

Having a strong social media presence can open many opportunities for your business and, once again, further establish your business as a leader in its industry. Social media allows your content to be shared by others, reposted by blogs and other news sources on social platforms. Often social media is the first impression that new customers/clients get of your business.

So what should you post, and how do you post? No, you don't need to create the next big trending TikTok dance (although it might help). What you need is a plan! Let's think again, **how do we inspire, educate and entertain?**

The strongest content is organic content. People love seeing you and your business behind the scenes and seeing an authentic representation of what you do. It's important to remember your brand and its voice, especially when writing captions. Make sure your social media content aligns with your company's voice, mission and vision. With that said, don't forget to have fun with it! Social media can be daunting at times, but it is indeed what you make of it.

We suggest creating themes! Themes make it easier for you to decide what type of content to post on certain days, times and even social media platforms. What you may post on Twitter, and Facebook may not be the same as what you post on LinkedIn and Instagram or TikTok. Remember that your audience will differ from platform to platform.

Non-Specific Social Media Content Ideas:

- **Guest Post / Carousel**
  If you stock products from brands, you can get the owners of those brands to do a guest post carousel. You can highlight some of the products and also highlight the owner.

- **Behind the Scenes**
  How your products are made? Let's get to know members of your team.

- **FAQ**
  It can consist of questions you frequently get from your customers. These questions can be designed into a template and posted as content.

- **Build User Generated Content**
  Share photos and content from your customers. Encourage your customers to share, tag, and hashtag pictures they take of your products. This helps you build your brand presence on social media platforms.

- **Giveaways**
  Build on the answers above and have users share photos to enter giveaways. Or, simply use a post as a monthly giveaway to have people follow, share and tag their friends into their posts.

- **Space Photos**
  Social media gives your audience an inside look into your retail experience without being in the store.

- **Product or Service Features**
  Use social media to showcase your products and do mini videos on features, services and/or products.

- **Create Guides**
  Guides are great educational posts to showcase and educate your audience. These guides could teach how to use your products, create shopping guides, or even guide things in your local hometown.

- **Interviews**
  Create unique features to interview local community members, your team members, and or customers. This can be an ongoing series of short and fun questions.

Engagement is also a huge part of social media marketing. Don't forget to reply to all your comments and engage with others on their feed. They took the time to write you, so you should take the time to write back. Never has there been a time when it has been so easy to connect with people worldwide.

SERVICE

Managing social media for your business is not always the most straightforward task. You may say to yourself: *"I run a dental clinic. What should I post, and when do I have the time?"* Well, you are not alone. It's essential to plan ahead and put together a schedule of themes and posts for you to get your social media on autopilot.

You may also say: *"Social media is not for me! It doesn't work for my industry."* You could say that, or you could take advantage of reaching millions of potential customers for free. Once you build an audience and a network of followers, they tell their friends and refer your service. Something makes your business unique, and you should tell the world.

Here are some ideas to help you get started:

- Video testimonials from clients/customers

- Tutorials or How To's at home

- Before / After images

- Showcase your team/staff

- Time Lapse and Process videos of the experience

- Showcase your office/clinic space

- Education

- Showcase your personal brand and journey

- Showcase neighbouring businesses and those that align with yours.

- Curate a staff music playlist

- Curate your team's favourite go to restaurants in and around your area

Twelve Tips!

- *Use a compilation of client testimonials as Facebook Ads.*

- *Trade services with a photographer to help you capture content and photos.*

RETAIL

There are endless opportunities to promote your business through social media with a retail business.

Let's say you are a Men's luxury clothing retailer. Give your user an internal look into your business, and help bring the products to life for them. Seeing products in use can frequently be enough to create a desire for someone to come make a purchase. People buy clothes to help make them feel a certain way. They want to feel good, look good and feel confident.

Here are some content ideas for your Men's Retail store:

- Post new products and new arrivals

- Use models to showcase the latest looks of the season

- Showing your products in action and how your customers can wear them for a night out.

- Educate your clientele on the brands you carry. What's so unique about each of them? Discuss how it's made, where it's from, and the concept behind the design.

- Create seasonal lookbooks where you can inspire your customers

- Invite fashion bloggers/content creators in store to try on and showcase your new arrivals and have them post on social media. Reuse the content and piggyback on their audience.

- Create a series where everyday customers are featured and what products they love.

- Talk about your personal brand (the owner), why you decided to open the business and why you are passionate about it. People LOVE hearing about the journey.

- Sponsor special events or local content creators looking for an outfit in exchange for them wearing your outfit for their night out. Reuse content from their photos.

- Sponsor outfits for a local or more prominent celebrity. E.g. the local sports star.

- Co-brand with other businesses or individuals for their photoshoots, e.g. men's grooming products or local business owners.

- Create and brand an interview series about the individuals/ ambassadors you partnered with, telling their stories about their journeys in life, career and business.

RESTAURANT

Who doesn't love food? How it's made, where it's sourced, how it's plated... there are tons of opportunities for social content when you're in the restaurant business! But just in case you're stuck on what to post, we've got you covered with a bit of a list of our own:

- **Post Pictures of Your Food**
  These can be individual dishes or a bountiful spread. We recommend finding the most mouthwatering angles of your food products and honing on that. It's all in the details.

- **Post Pictures of Drinks**
  Promote your drinks with ambient photos of your thirst-quenching beverages and how each cocktail is made.

- **Make Instagram Reels or Videos of Food Being Made**
  Seeing how the food is made is a great way to entice people! Whether new customers or regulars, seeing a video of delicious food being made will definitely hit them in their cravings. Think of Salt Bae... his restaurant Nusr-Et gained popularity from his extravagant meat cutting videos.

- **Post Your Specials and Featured Items**
  Margherita Pizzas on Monday? Sangria special on Wednesday? Promote your specials on your socials with tasty imagery and catchy captions!

- **Post Pictures of Your Staff**
  Meet the people behind the experience! Introducing yourself and your staff on socials makes your business seem more friendly and approachable.

- **New/Seasonal Food Items**
  whether it's green beers on St. Patrick's Day, a Christmas roast for the holidays or a fresh new gelato flavour to beat the heat, get your fans

and followers into the season!

- **Invite your Customers to Create New Menu Items**
  Customers love to give feedback. Invite them to give their best ideas for your next menu feature.

Twelve Tip!

Create merchandise for your restaurant and use it as props in your photos or giveaways. E.g. mugs, Hats, t-shirts, cooking aprons.

CHAPTER 9
EXCHANGE SERVICES
You Scratch My Back, I'll Scratch Yours

Ah, bartering. A lost skill in today's modern world. Bartering goods and services is one of the earliest forms of commerce! Before money, humans long exchanged goods and services via the bartering system.

One of the best ways to get out there and exchange services is to **leverage exposure.** Exchanging services must be done in communication and agreement with your counterparts. If not approached correctly, the exchange can seem one-sided. Always create a W3 situation, a **win-win-win situation**— one win for the customer of both businesses, one win for the business you partner with and finally, a win for your business! You can not only exchange directly for marketing and exchange services but also for future marketing use.

Suppose you are a new graphic designer. Approach your favourite glasses shop and help them design a new logo in exchange for a new pair of glasses. You can now use this exchange to leverage your latest portfolio piece and market it to get more clients for the optical shop. The optical shop wins once more by having a fantastic brand you created, thus attracting more customers.

SERVICE

A great way to exchange services for a practice is to sponsor an event to get exposure. Is there a sporting event happening in your city? This is a perfect opportunity to set up some massage tables or physiotherapy tables and help athletes recover on the spot. You get your name out there and provide your services at an event and leave each person with a small grab bag or gift from your business.

A great example would be the annual **Lululemon** 10K Race in Edmonton, Canada. There are physio and massage practices that sponsor the event and set up their booths to help athletes recover whenever it is hosted.

Remember, it doesn't necessarily have to be a cross-city marathon event. It can be a golf tournament, local basketball or hockey tournament, or any trade show, conference or special event.

As a hair salon or studio, you can call for models or volunteers. This allows the hairstylists to experiment and try new methods while also creating content for them to post.

RETAIL

Looking to show off your merchandise? A model call is a great way to trade services. As a retail store, you can call models or content creators to help spread the message in exchange for merchandise or product.

You can post a roll call for a specific look and exchange your product for modeling use. This helps you market by allowing you to have models for photoshoots and reach new audiences through your models.

This can also work as customers help spread the word. You can exchange products for them to model or showcase your merchandise in exchange for your business or for them to post on social media or use for advertising.

RESTAURANT

Who doesn't love food? Food bloggers and content creators are an excellent way for restaurants to exchange services. The direct exchange is food for blog posts. Food bloggers are always looking for new restaurants to try, and you can invite them for a meal on the house in exchange for a blog or social post. **Use influencers/bloggers and creators from diverse circles to reach and attract their specific audiences.** You can stack the exposure by creating special giveaways that grow engagement and following through Like and Share contests.

Remember, word of mouth is one of the most critical parts of building a successful hospitality experience. Always treat your guests with the best service possible. Your food and service will keep them coming back and spread the word.

Twelve Tip!

Work with the host to create a system to find who is new into the restaurant, mark their table with either a separate colour napkin or floral arrangement or cutlery. Ensure your manager does rounds asking about their experience, and reward your new group with a coupon for a drink or dessert on their next visit. This will help keep them coming back with new hungry mouths next time!

CHAPTER 10

BRANDING IS A FEELING

Building Brand and Culture Through Your Best Fans

Brand awareness is the first step in our customer journey. It lays the foundation for building a trusting relationship with your customers. Branding is also responsible for how familiar your target audience is with your business. We can see how branding works in two main areas:

Top of Mind

Just as it sounds, top of mind brand awareness is the automatic association of a brand to a specific product of service. It is the brand that comes off the top of your mind whenever it's industry is mentioned. Who comes to the top of your mind when we say "soda company?" Coke Cola? Pepsi? The stronger your company's branding, the more awareness and the higher chance of creating a company to be remembered.

Aided Recall

Aided Recall is the type of brand awareness that occurs when seeing a recognizable brand element, TV commercial or an online ad that prompts a clue or triggers a memory recalling a specific brand.

Branding is a feeling. It is responsible for the feelings and associations you create for your customers when they hear about your brand. What feelings, senses or memories come to mind when we think about Starbucks Coffee, Mercedes-Benz or Apple? Do you suddenly recall the smell of coffee? Are you reminded of luxury? Did you think about your latest visit to the Genius Bar?

Brand awareness creates equity, higher perceived values, and fosters loyalty. Creating equity means being memorable, creating social value and ensuring you are recognizable. Customers are willing to pay more for your product/service with a Higher Perceived Value. Loyalty means customers will choose you above the others, return, and recommend you to others. This is why people are willing to pay $1500 for an iPhone or $7 for a Starbucks Coffee.

Excellent brand awareness builds associations. When in need of a cotton swab, do you think of Q-Tip? What about facial tissue? Kleenex. Looking up something online? Google it.

Remember that people support brands they LIKE, KNOW and TRUST. Building brand and culture helps your customers and loyal fans market for you. They are waiting for the latest and greatest news, your next product release, or they can't wait to share the newest item they buy from you. Think about Nike, Air Jordans and how they have a cult-like following.

"People don't buy what you do, they buy why you do it" - **Simon Sinek, Author of *"Start With Why."***

SERVICE

Treat your regular customers like royalty. Membership packages can help you do just that! When you provide value to your customers, they will keep returning and bring others with them.

Are there some tools your customer can purchase from you that you can use as merchandise? For example, if you are a physiotherapy clinic, can you create branded foam rollers for your clients to purchase? This can even be an excellent opportunity for collaboration or gifts to keep your brand top of mind.

For dental clinics, you can co-brand a toothbrush for giveaways. As a marketing agency, we are creating this book to share with our audience in this case scenario!

RETAIL

Creating an exclusive member group can help create scarcity for your product. Provide exclusive access, discounts, and first picks to your members. Many retailers have an unspoken rule that provides this to customers who regularly spend over a certain amount. Build a club and create special merchandise, e.g. a Hat or t-shirt that only club members can access. This can also be access to first-in-line sales, product offerings, or complimentary special events that only special members can access.

We have also seen some of our favourite clothing retailers create their own fashion lines to build an in-house brand. Not only does this take merch to the next level, but it makes an accessible in-house brand your audience can support. This can help you increase your margins and build your brand for the long term.

RESTAURANT

Some restaurant merch pairings can be executed exceptionally well. Get creative with illustrations and sayings from your restaurant. Or, to be even more unique, try creating signature scented products (turn your signature lavender honey latte into a scented candle). What places can you recall having a signature scent? E.g. Home Depot iconically smells like fresh sawdust. The Renaissance Hotel by Marriott Bonvoy has been known to brand its lobby's smell. You can even buy it and use it in your own home.

Work with a local graphic artist or designer to create a unique line of merchandise for your restaurant, one of the many possible collectibles for your raving fans.

We included this great list that Esquire magazine put together of some fun merch projects companies worldwide have executed - Check it out at https://bit.ly/3sxjxNp.

People always want to be part of the "club." Can you make a punch pass or virtual punch pass that creates rewards for customers? These small value providers keep your customers coming back and keep that word of mouth going.

BE CURIOUS, CRAFT
YOUR STORY, BUILD
YOUR BRAND AND
REMEMBER TO BE
AUTHENTIC.

-ERIC CHENG

CLOSING REMARKS

Congratulations! You've made it to the end...of this book! Now the real hard work begins as the next steps of your next journey await. It's never easy to take the first step (or any step forward), and it's okay to take one step backward to take three steps ahead. As a marketer/entrepreneur, you know that there are highs and lows and that things work and don't work, but that's okay. We get you. The journey is never easy, no matter what business you are in and your role. What's important is that you continue to focus on your goals. The path for success and fulfilling one's dreams will never be straightforward. The ups and downs and the winding road lead to real growth. Besides, where's the fun in easy?

We've covered a lot and every business will operate differently. No business is alike as there are no two customers who are alike. Marketing and branding are about understanding your customer. I mean really understanding your customer. You have to understand what makes them "feel" a certain way when they interact with your product, business or brand. This positive feeling they get is what becomes brand loyalty. Be sure to always make your audience and customer the hero. They took the time to choose you! Out of all the possibilities in the world, they chose you. Take the time to build long-lasting relationships with your audience. **It takes 5X more in advertising and marketing than retaining and growing an existing customer.**

The marketing landscape and the technology being used are ever-changing, but your goals and dream have not. Don't be afraid to try new things. Think out of the box and experiment with new ways to interact and market with your audience. We live in a time where opportunities and technology to help us market our brand are so easily accessible and endless. Take advantage of the present to help you write your future. Growth only begins when you start moving out of your comfort zone.